Presentation Skills

Captivate and educate your audience

Fourth Edition

Steve Mandel

A Crisp Fifty-Minute™ Series Book

AXZO  PRESS

Presentation Skills

Captivate and educate your audience

Fourth Edition

Steve Mandel

CREDITS:

President, Axzo Press:	**Jon Winder**
Vice President, Product Development:	**Charles G. Blum**
Vice President, Operations:	**Josh Pincus**
Director, Publishing Systems Development:	**Dan Quackenbush**
Developmental Editor:	**Jim O'Shea**
Copy Editor:	**Catherine E. Oliver**

Trademarks

Crisp Fifty-Minute Series is a trademark of Axzo Press.

Some of the product names and company names used in this book have been used for identification purposes only and may be trademarks or registered trademarks of their respective manufacturers and sellers.

Disclaimer

We reserve the right to revise this publication and make changes from time to time in its content without notice.

ISBN 10: 1-4260-0487-7
ISBN 13: 978-1-4260-0487-2
Printed in the United States of America
1 2 3 4 5 6 7 8 9 11 10 09

Table of Contents

Appendix 77

About the Author

Steve Mandel, founder of Mandel Communications, is a nationally known training consultant and lecturer specializing in presentation skills training. Since 1984, his company has trained salespeople, executives, engineers, and managers in the skills necessary to effectively present their ideas. Mandel Communications has delivered programs in more than 40 countries and provides workshops in numerous languages.

Mr. Mandel is the author of two Crisp Series books, *Great Presentations* (formerly *Effective Presentation Skills)* and *Technical Presentation Skills*, as well as numerous articles. He has been a featured speaker for organizations on the topic of management communication skills in the professional environment.

A two-day workshop based on the material in this book is available from Mandel Communications. For more information, please contact:

Mandel Communications, Inc.
820 Bay Avenue, Suite 113
Capitola, CA 95010
1-800-262-6335
www.mandelcom.com
smandel@mandelcom.com

Dedication

This book is dedicated to those who helped make it happen and without whose support it would not exist: my wonderful wife, Carol, my children, Joe, Paul, and Alex, and all my colleagues at Mandel Communications.

To the Reader

There is a myth that great speakers are "born, not made," that certain individuals have the innate ability to stand in front of an audience with no anxiety and give a moving, dynamic speech. Well, that just isn't so!

People we consider great speakers have usually spent years developing and practicing their craft. They had to start at the beginning and learn the basics of organization, preparation, delivery, and anxiety management. Once the basics were in hand, they needed to continue to build on their abilities.

Professional athletes constantly practice the basics because they know that without such practice, they will not excel. To an outsider, the thought of a professional golfer spending hour after hour practicing the basics might seem ridiculous. But to that professional, the continued mastery of those basic skills is the very foundation of success.

Learning to be a better speaker is similar to learning any activity. In the beginning, it can be frustrating. After a few lessons, in which you learn some theory and practice some of the basic techniques, skills usually improve. Learning to do anything well takes constant practice and mastery of the basics.

Speaking is no different. Before becoming comfortable as a speaker, you need to learn some basic skills and then actively seek opportunities to practice those skills. This might mean walking into your manager's office and volunteering to give more presentations, or joining a speaking club that allows you to speak in an organized setting. The more experience you gain, the more proficient and comfortable you will become.

Good luck!

Steve Mandel

Preface

The study of how to give effective speeches dates back to ancient Greece. Around 350 BC, Aristotle wrote his famous *Rhetoric*, now considered to be one of the finest formal books on the subject. Now, 2300 years later, we are still struggling with the same problems that the Greeks encountered and that speakers have grappled with throughout the ages.

The advent of technology has both complicated and simplified the task of the speaker. For example, today it is possible to produce complex graphs on a computer, display them digitally with a projector, and present them via the Internet. But how much information should be put on that graph? And most important, where does that graph fit into the organizational plan (if there is one) of the presentation as a whole?

This book answers the fundamental questions of how to prepare and deliver a great presentation. Proven techniques are provided to help readers learn the skills needed to give more confident, enthusiastic, and persuasive presentations. Topics covered include how to use body language effectively, how to organize ideas and data for maximum impact, how to develop and use slides and other visuals, and (of course) how to deliver what you have prepared.

This book provides some theory, but more often presents simple and practical suggestions on giving more effective presentations. In this fourth edition, I have added more information on how to best organize a presentation, and I have updated the material on technology and the use of slides.

Definitions

The terms "speech" and "presentation" are often used interchangeably. For our purposes, it is useful to understand the difference.

A presentation is a type of speech. Typically, when we think of a speech, we think of a dedication speech, a political speech, a speech of tribute, or some similar event that is more public in nature than a presentation might be.

Presentations are speeches that are usually given in a business, technical, professional, or scientific environment. The audience is likely to be more specialized than the audience attending a typical speech event.

This book leans toward helping those who give presentations. Because a presentation is a type of speech, however, there are ideas and skills in this book that will also be helpful to any speech-maker.

Learning Objectives

Complete this book, and you'll know how to:

1) Evaluate your skill and build confidence as a speaker

2) Prepare the content of a successful presentation

3) Use presentation technology to your advantage

4) Prepare yourself and the room for a successful presentation

5) Deliver a presentation well

Workplace and Management Competencies Mapping

For over 30 years, business and industry have used competency models to select employees. The trend toward using competency-based approaches in the education, training, assessment, and development of workers has emerged more recently within the Employment and Training Administration (ETA), a division of the United States Department of Labor.

The ETA's General Competency Model Framework spans a wide array of competencies, from the more basic ones, such as reading and writing, to more advanced occupation-specific competencies. The Crisp Series finds its home in what the ETA refers to as the Workplace Competencies and the Management Competencies.

Presentation Skills covers information vital to mastering the following competencies:

Workplace Competencies:

▶ Planning and Organizing

▶ Working with Tools and Technology

Management Competencies:

▶ Informing

For a comprehensive mapping of Crisp Series titles to the Workplace and Management competencies, visit www.CrispSeries.com.

About the Crisp 50-Minute Series

The Crisp 50-Minute Series was designed to cover critical business and professional development topics in the shortest possible time. Our easy-to-read, easy-to-understand format can be used for self-study or for classroom training. With a wealth of hands-on exercises, the 50-Minute books keep you engaged and help you retain critical skills.

What You Need to Know

We designed the Crisp 50-Minute Series to be as self-explanatory as possible. But there are a few things you should know before you begin the book.

Exercises

Exercises look like this:

EXERCISE TITLE

Questions and other information would be here.

Keep a pencil handy. Any time you see an exercise, you should try to complete it. If the exercise has specific answers, an answer key will be provided in the appendix. (Some exercises ask you to think about your own opinions or situation; these types of exercises will not have answer keys.)

Forms

A heading like this means that the rest of the page is a form:

FORMHEAD

Forms are meant to be reusable. You might want to make a photocopy of a form before you fill it out, so that you can use it again later.

A Note to Instructors

We've tried to make the Crisp 50-Minute Series books as useful as possible as classroom training manuals. Here are some of the features we provide for instructors:

- ▶ PowerPoint presentations
- ▶ Answer keys
- ▶ Assessments
- ▶ Customization

PowerPoint Presentations

You can download a PowerPoint presentation for this book from our Web site at www.CrispSeries.com.

Answer keys

If an exercise has specific answers, an answer key will be provided in the appendix. (Some exercises ask you to think about your own opinions or situation; these types of exercises will not have answer keys.)

Assessments

For each 50-Minute Series book, we have developed a 35- to 50-item assessment. The assessment for this book is available at www.CrispSeries.com. *Assessments should not be used in any employee-selection process.*

Customization

Crisp books can be quickly and easily customized to meet your needs—from adding your logo to developing proprietary content. Crisp books are available in print and electronic form. For more information on customization, see www.CrispSeries.com.

Assessing

Your Skills

> *Honesty is an active verb, not a passive noun. Go out of your way to be truthful, beginning with the things that you say to yourself."*
>
> **–Joe Tye, Values Coach America**

In this part:

- ▶ Evaluating Yourself
- ▶ Dealing with Anxiety
- ▶ Tips for Reducing Anxiety
- ▶ Turning Your Assessment into a Plan

Evaluating Yourself

To be a more effective presenter, you'll find it useful to examine your current skills. The following exercises can help you determine which areas to focus on to increase your confidence and competence as a presenter.

ASSESS YOUR COMFORT LEVEL

Check the category that best describes you as a speaker:

❑ **Avoider** An avoider does everything possible to steer clear of having to get in front of an audience. Avoiders might even seek careers that do not involve making presentations.

❑ **Resister** A resister has fear when asked to speak. This fear may be strong. Resisters might not be able to avoid speaking as part of their jobs, but they never encourage it. When they do speak, they do so with great reluctance and considerable pain.

❑ **Accepter** The accepter will give presentations as part of the job but doesn't seek those opportunities. Accepters occasionally give a presentation and feel as though they did a good job. They even find that once in a while, they are quite persuasive and enjoy speaking in front of a group.

❑ **Seeker** A seeker looks for opportunities to speak. The seeker understands that anxiety can be a stimulant which fuels enthusiasm during a presentation. Seekers work at building their professional communication skills and self-confidence by speaking often.

ASSESS YOUR CURRENT PRESENTATION SKILLS

Please read each statement and circle the number that best describes you: 5 represents "Always" and 1 means "Never." Then add the circled numbers to discover your overall score. During the rest of this book, concentrate on those items you marked 1, 2, or 3.

Statements	Always – Never
1. I thoroughly analyze my audience.	5 4 3 2 1
2. I determine the key objectives before planning a presentation.	5 4 3 2 1
3. I write down my core message first in order to build a presentation around it.	5 4 3 2 1
4. I incorporate both a preview and a review of the main ideas as I organize my presentation.	5 4 3 2 1
5. I develop my core message so that it will catch the attention of my audience and still provide the necessary background information.	5 4 3 2 1
6. My conclusion refers to my core message and contains a call to action.	5 4 3 2 1
7. The visual and graphics I use are carefully prepared, simple, and easy to read and have impact.	5 4 3 2 1
8. The number of visuals and graphics I use will enhance, not detract, from my presentation.	5 4 3 2 1
9. I use both energy and composure in delivering a presentation.	5 4 3 2 1
10. I ensure that the benefits suggested to my audience are clear and compelling.	5 4 3 2 1
11. I communicate ideas with enthusiasm.	5 4 3 2 1
12. I rehearse so there is a minimum focus on notes and maximum attention paid to my audience.	5 4 3 2 1
13. My notes contain only key words, so I avoid reading from a manuscript or technical paper.	5 4 3 2 1

CONTINUED

14. My presentations are rehearsed standing up and using my visuals.   5 4 3 2 1

15. I prepare answers to anticipated questions, and practice responding to them.   5 4 3 2 1

16. I arrange seating (if appropriate) and check audio-visual equipment before the presentation.   5 4 3 2 1

17. I maintain good eye contact with the audience at all times.   5 4 3 2 1

18. My gestures are natural and not constrained by anxiety.   5 4 3 2 1

19. My voice is strong and clear and is not a monotone.   5 4 3 2 1

TOTAL SCORE: _____

Set Your Goals

If your total score in this exercise was:

90–95	You have the qualities of an excellent presenter.
70–89	You are above average but could improve in some areas.
Below 69	This course should help you.

What Do You Want to Achieve?

Using the information from this exercise, check those boxes that indicate goals you would like to achieve.

I hope to:

❏ Understand the anxiety I feel before a presentation and learn how to use it constructively during my presentation.

❏ Learn how to organize my thoughts and data in a logical and concise manner.

❏ Develop the skills necessary to communicate enthusiasm about the ideas I present, and develop a more dynamic presentation style.

❏ Transform question-and-answer sessions into an enjoyable and productive part of the presentation process.

❏ Construct visual aids that have impact, and use them effectively during my presentation.

Dealing with Anxiety

Anxiety is a natural state that occurs any time we are placed under stress. For most people, giving a presentation causes some degree of stress! When this type of stress occurs, physiological changes take place that may cause symptoms such as:

▶ A nervous stomach

▶ Sweating

▶ Tremors in the hands and legs

▶ Accelerated breathing

▶ Increased heart rate

Don't worry! If you have any of these symptoms before or during a presentation, you are normal. If none of these things happen, you are one in a million. Almost everyone experiences some stress before presentations, even when the task is something simple like, "tell the group something about yourself." The trick is to make your excess energy work for you.

When you learn to make stress work for you, it can be the fuel for a more enthusiastic and dynamic presentation. The next few pages will teach you how to recycle your stress in a positive form that will help you become a better presenter.

As someone once said, "The trick is to get those butterflies in your stomach to fly in one direction!"

Paul

Paul is an engineer with a robotics company. In two weeks, he has to deliver a major presentation to managers from several divisions in his company, on a project he is proposing. He knows his topic, but his audience will be examining his proposal very closely, and Paul is certain he will receive some very tough questions. Every time Paul thinks about planning what to say, he gets too nervous to begin work.

If Paul's problem of anxiety before a presentation sounds familiar, then the following tips may help.

Tips for Reducing Anxiety

Organize

Lack of organization is one of the major causes of anxiety. Later in this book, you will learn a simple process for organizing your presentation. Knowing that your thoughts are well organized will give you more confidence, which will allow you to focus your energy on your presentation.

Visualize

Imagine walking into a room, being introduced, delivering your presentation with enthusiasm, fielding questions with confidence, and leaving the room knowing you did a great job. Mentally rehearse this sequence with all the details of your particular situation, and it will help you focus on what you need to do to be successful.

Practice

Many speakers rehearse a presentation mentally or with just their lips. Instead, you should practice standing up, as if an audience were in front of you, and use your visual aids (if you have them). At least two dress rehearsals are recommended. If possible, have somebody critique the first one and/or have it videotaped. Watch the playback, listen to the critique, and incorporate any changes you think are required before your final practice session. There is no better preparation than this.

Carol

Carol is an account executive with a children's book publisher. She has been asked to present the sales figures for her region at the company's national sales meeting. Her colleague Nancy is finishing her remarks, and in two minutes, Carol will have to stand up and make her presentation. She is experiencing extreme anxiety at a time when she needs to be focused and collected.

Carol's situation is quite common. If you experience anxiety immediately before speaking, try some of the following exercises next time you're waiting for your turn to stand up and speak.

Breathe

When your muscles tighten and you feel nervous, you might not be breathing deeply enough. The first thing to do is to sit up, erect but relaxed, and inhale deeply a number of times.

Focus on Relaxing

Instead of thinking about the tension, focus on relaxing. As you breathe, tell yourself on the inhale, "I am," and on the exhale, "relaxed." Try to clear your mind of everything except the repetition of the "I am…relaxed" statement, and continue this exercise for several minutes.

Release Tension

As tension increases and your muscles tighten, nervous energy can get locked into the limbs. This unreleased energy may cause your hands and legs to shake. Before you stand up to give a presentation, it's a good idea to try to release some of this pent-up tension by doing a simple, unobtrusive isometric exercise.

Starting with your toes and calf muscles, and moving up through your body, tighten your muscles, finally making a fist (i.e., toes, feet, calves, thighs, stomach, chest, shoulders, arms, and fingers). Immediately release all of the tension and take a deep breath. Repeat this exercise until you feel the tension start to drain away. Remember, this exercise is to be done quietly so that no one knows you're relaxing!

Joe

Joe is an accountant with a major financial organization. When he gives presentations, he gets very nervous. He sweats, his hands tremble, and his voice becomes a monotone (and at times inaudible). He also fidgets with items, such as a pen, and looks at his notes or the overhead projector screen, not at his audience. He can barely wait to finish and return to his seat.

Joe's plight is not uncommon. You might not have all of these symptoms, but you can probably relate to some of them. The following techniques will help you in situations where you get nervous while speaking.

Move

Speakers who stand in one spot and never gesture, experience tension. In order to relax, you need to release tension by allowing your muscles to flex. If you find you are locking your arms in one position when you speak, then practice releasing them so they do the same thing they would if you were in an animated one-on-one conversation. You can't gesture too much if it is natural.

Make Eye Contact with the Audience

Give your presentation to one person at a time. Relate with your audience as individuals. Look in peoples' eyes as you speak. Connect with people. Make it personal and personable. The eye contact should help you relax because you become less isolated from the audience and learn to react to their interest in you.

Remember, the more the presentation is like a conversation, the more comfortable you and the audience will be

Turning Your Assessment into a Plan

Check those items you intend to practice and incorporate in future presentations you make.

I plan to:

❑ Organize my material.

❑ Visualize myself delivering a successful presentation.

❑ Rehearse by standing up and using all of my visual aids.

❑ Breathe deeply just before speaking and during my presentation.

❑ Focus on relaxing with simple, unobtrusive isometric techniques.

❑ Release my tension in a positive way by directing it to my audience.

❑ Move when I speak, to stay relaxed and natural.

❑ Maintain good eye contact with my audience.

2

Planning Your Presentation

"*It takes one hour of preparation for each minute of presentation time.*"

—Wayne Burgraff

In this part:

▶ Clarifying Your Strategy

▶ Six Steps to Planning Your Presentation

▶ Some Thoughts on Using Handouts

▶ Preparing for Your Next Presentation

Clarifying Your Strategy

Can you imagine your company or organization having no strategy in place, and only executing tactics on a short-term basis? It would not be in existence too long if it did that. Likewise, we need a strong strategy in place first in order to make a presentation effective.

Frequently, presenters "organize" their presentations by creating a PowerPoint slide show. Without a unifying strategy and a clearly stated core message, however, the slides may lead to a muddied message and unclear focus and direction.

Clarifying a strategy and a core message will lead to a much stronger and more effective presentation. You can do this by following these six steps:

1. Analyze the objectives.

2. Develop an understanding of the audience.

3. Clarify the core message.

4. Plan the main and supporting ideas.

5. Develop "color spots" to help the audience remember the message.

6. Build a strong finish.

You are now ready to build your presentation into a coherent whole—and to assemble your ideas into a clear and compelling plan. The process is very straightforward and very powerful. It is based on research that tells us the best ways to maximize information retention and, when we need to, influence others.

Definitions: _Unless noted otherwise, the word "slides" refers to visuals created with Microsoft PowerPoint or any of the other presentation software packages currently available._

Six Steps to Planning Your Presentation

Step 1: Analyze Presentation Objectives

It is important to be clear about what exactly you are trying to accomplish in your presentation. Before moving forward, answer the following questions.

▶ What do I want to achieve by making this presentation?

_____

_____

▶ What do I want my audience to do and think during my presentation?

_____

_____

▶ What specific things do I want my audience to do after my presentation?

_____

_____

▶ How do I want my audience to feel about my subject matter after the presentation?

_____

_____

▶ How do I want my audience to perceive me and my organization?

_____

_____

Step 2: Understand Your Audience

Put yourself in the shoes of the people who will be listening to your presentation. When analyzing your audience, you have five things to consider:

Needs

It's important to find out before the presentation what the group thinks it needs—this might be quite different from what you thought. You might inquire about the group's needs beforehand, or if appropriate, ask members of the audience about their needs and expectations before the presentation.

Attitude

How do your audience members feel about the topic? Are they positive, neutral, or negative on the subject? Is the group's opinion mixed? Are certain sections of the presentation likely to generate strong feelings in either direction? What you uncover here must be factored into the structure and phrasing of the presentation.

Knowledge Level

All of us have our own areas of specialization. Speakers must be careful not to use technical language, idiomatic expressions, or slang for non-native English-speaking audiences, or abbreviations, acronyms, buzzwords, and other jargon that people might not understand. If in doubt, ask the audience if they are familiar with the relevant terminology, and define words and phrases if necessary.

Environment

Consider the room and general environment in which you will be speaking. Could seating, room size, equipment availability, and lighting affect your interaction with the audience? Environment can also be thought of in psychological terms. Is there anything emotional or psychological that might affect your audience's reception of you and your ideas? The psychological environment could be affected by recent good or bad news—the company just landed a huge contract, for example, or announced an imminent downsizing.

Demographic Information

This information can include the age, sex, race, religion, culture, and language of the audience members. Of these, culture and language present the greatest challenge to speakers. If you're delivering presentations to international audiences, it's a good idea to gain an understanding of any cultural differences that might affect the way in which you present. Also, you might need to understand the language level of your audience—some members might not be native speakers of the language you are using. Find out in advance if you need an interpreter.

AUDIENCE ANALYSIS WORKSHEET

This form should help you plan more efficiently for any presentation.

1. The specific needs of the audience members are:

   _____

   _____

   _____

2. Their attitude toward the topic is:

   _____

   _____

   _____

3. The knowledge level of the audience in relation to the subject matter is:

   _____

   _____

   _____

4. The physical and psychological environmental elements that might affect the audience are:

   _____

   _____

   _____

5. The audience demographic factors that might affect your presentation are:

   _____

   _____

   _____

This page may be reproduced without additional permission from the publisher.

Step 3: Clarify Your Core Message by Using SCIPAB

After clarifying your objectives and doing a thorough audience analysis, and before developing the body of the presentation or any slides, clarify the core message of your presentation. To do this, develop sentences for the following six areas, which you can remember with the abbreviation "SCIPAB":

Situation

Complication

Implication

Position

Action

Benefit

Elevator Pitch

These six sentences constitute what is commonly known as the "elevator pitch"— a clear, concise statement of the core message of your presentation. It is what you might say to your boss on a quick elevator ride when he asks you to tell him about your upcoming presentation. Preparing the pitch first gives you an important focal point before moving forward to the main body of the presentation, and it's a critical step to success.

Use this method regardless of the type of presentation you are giving. It works equally well for informational or scientific presentations as it does for sales presentations.

This critical part of your presentation is assembled with only six sentences. If it gets longer, the sharp focus you create will be lost and its potential impact on the audience will be diminished.

Here are explanations and examples for each sentence of SCIPAB:

Situation: This sentence describes the present situation, adding your insight and understanding of the current business and/or technical environment. The information provided in this sentence should be known by your audience and accepted as a "given." It describes the status quo and is non-controversial in that the audience will most likely agree with it.

Example: *"Our business has grown by 30% in the last two years."*

Complication: This sentence describes the challenges or drawbacks of the situation, any obstacles created by the situation, and any related business or technical risks. The information provided in this sentence can be new and/or controversial for your audience.

Example: *"Because of this growth, we have outgrown our computer systems."*

Implication: This sentence addresses the consequences to your audience of failing to act on the issues raised in the complication. This vital element answers the audience's "so what" question, providing both a logical transition to and a sense of urgency about your core message.

Example: *"If we don't update our systems, our growth will come to a halt."*

Position: This sentence tells the audience what you personally think about the topic. It's your stance, your opinion, your thesis, your belief about the issue. It must be stated clearly and succinctly. It's important to put this information out at the start of the presentation; it tells the audience exactly where you stand so they won't be wondering what the presentation is all about (as many audiences do!).

Example: *"A major upgrade and overhaul of our entire IT system would be very good for our company."*

Action: This is simply a statement of what you would like your audience to do, to believe, or to understand. There is a wide range of "actions" an audience might take. At the start of the presentation (opening action), tell the audience what you want them to do or think during the presentation. At the end of the presentation (closing action), tell them what you want them to do as a next step.

Opening action example: *"Please consider my proposal today for a major update of our network."*

Closing action example: *"I'd like to get your approval for funding the network overhaul by the end of this week so we can begin work."*

Benefit: This sentence tells the audience what is in it for them if they do what you ask. Benefits can be for the organization, the individual, or both.

Example: *"By updating our network, we will be able to continue our growth and ensure our system's security and stability."*

Putting It All Together

Using the SCIPAB method is the best way to open your presentation. Research shows that putting your core message right up front is the strongest way to eliminate ambiguity and move your presentation forward.

For maximum impact, plan on delivering the SCIPAB with no slide on the screen. A slide at this point would decrease the impact of this concise and important part of your presentation.

Presentation Tip: *It is typical to have a title slide on the screen as the presentation starts. In PowerPoint, you can temporarily black it out by pressing "B" on the keyboard as you deliver your SCIPAB. This blacks out the screen in Slide Show view.*

The second slide can be an agenda slide. You can display it by pressing any letter key to remove the black-out effect and then pressing the Enter key to change the slide.

Step 4: Plan the Main and Supporting Ideas

Now you must decide upon the key information areas you want to cover in your presentation. Using Post-It® notes, note cards, or a similar tool, brainstorm some possible ideas for your presentation. Write one idea on each Post-It. Let the ideas flow at this point; do not edit—that will come later. The strategy is to generate as many ideas as possible.

Once you have a large number of ideas, you'll want to focus your content on what matters most to the audience. Put aside any ideas that are not germane to your audience, and any ideas that could be shared in handouts and other forms of communication.

The Rule of Three

Take the remaining ideas and group them into common themes. When developing your presentation, try to follow the Rule of Three by organizing your content around no more than three main ideas. This easy-to-follow pattern makes for a clearer presentation and increases audience retention of critical information.

These three main ideas are the general assertions you plan to make to your audience. Supporting ideas can consist of facts, explanations, analyses, technical data, references, stories, analogies, or other forms of evidence that support your main idea.

Logical Flow

Using the information you've gathered, build a logical flow in your presentation. Try different arrangements to see what will work best. Always keep your audience analysis in mind.

In the actual presentation, after you state your SCIPAB, you will preview your main ideas for the audience. For example, "Today we will first cover the nature of the problems with our old computer systems; then we will discuss the benefits of an updated system. And finally, we will look at how we would implement the new system with minimal disruption to our business." Then the supporting ideas, and their discussion, will make up the bulk of time spent in the presentation.

Step 5: Develop Color Spots

Now you face a challenge—most of your listeners will hear many important messages in any given week or month, so one of your key concerns is making sure that your information is remembered. You have created the logical flow of the information in the presentation, and you now need to bring it alive and increase the audience's attention, comprehension, and retention of your message. It's not enough that your message is well designed; you must also make it memorable.

Engage Your Listeners

I call this process "adding color." The purpose of "adding color" to your presentation is to engage your listeners, help them make connections, and give them a strong sense that the information you are sharing is focused on them and their needs.

Here are some of the ways you can "add color" to your messages to help ensure that the ideas and solutions are remembered after the doors close on the meeting and your listeners have moved on to the next task:

▶ **Use slides and other visuals such as whiteboards or demos.** Slides are the most commonly used color spot. Remember that the real purpose of a slide is to make it easier for listeners to "get it." Avoid complex graphics or word-heavy charts. Save those for the speaker notes or supplementary slides to be handed out but not displayed on the screen. Consider using whiteboards and demos in addition to slides if appropriate.

▶ **Plan for moments of interaction.** Consider using a series of well-planned questions to guide your listeners to the points you want to make. With larger groups in which actual participation may not be possible, use rhetorical questions to engage the audience.

▶ **Tell stories.** Personal stories, or business stories from your personal experience, pack a big punch. The twofold benefit is that if you have lived the story, you have the passion to tell it well, and you won't forget the punch line! To your listeners, a well-told story is interesting and memorable; it helps to establish your credibility. Remember, stories need to be short, and they must make a relevant point!

▶ **Use analogies.** The power of an analogy is that it helps a person understand a new concept by relating it to something that is already familiar. Think of how the term "information super-highway" initially helped people understand the evolution of the digital age. Don't worry about the perfect analogy; "close enough" will work. Analogies are particularly useful for explaining technical processes to a non-technical audience.

► **Use humor.** Humor is a wonderful rapport builder. Avoid telling jokes, however—they can often be misunderstood or can be offensive to audience members. If you even ask yourself, "Should I tell that joke," don't! The best humor often happens spontaneously, in the moment when you quit taking yourself so seriously and have fun with the audience.

► **Refer to current events.** Scanning newspapers, Internet news, business news, and technology reports can provide rich color spots for a presentation.

► **Use quotes and statistics.** Again, choose those resources that will gain the respect of your listeners. The value of a quote is that it can become a "sound bite"—a memorable phrase that will remain with listeners long after the completion of the presentation. Carefully chosen sources also add to the credibility of your message, because "someone else" said it instead of you.

Whether you are giving a technical presentation, selling software, or giving a business presentation of any type, adding listener-focused color spots will engage your audience, give listeners the sense that your presentation really is "all about them," and ultimately, result in better retention of your facts and information.

Like the spots on a butterfly's wings, color spots in a presentation are both immensely useful and add interest.

Step 6: Build a Strong Finish

This step has two parts: first review the main ideas, and then restate the core message.

Review the Main Ideas

Before proceeding to the final statements, review the main ideas you have covered for the audience. Using the example from the preview earlier, you can say something like, *"Today we have covered the nature of the problems with our old computer system and the benefits of an updated system. Now, we will look at how we could implement the new system with minimal disruption to our business."*

Restate the Core Message

Make your presentation end on a strong note! This is best accomplished by repeating the central core message put forth at the beginning of the presentation. This message consists of the PAB portion of the original SCIPAB. The only change is that the closing action will now tell the audience what you want them to do after the presentation. In other words, the closing action now specifies the next steps.

Some Thoughts on Using Handouts

Typically, audiences want copies of the slides you are using. Audience members will use these to follow along and take notes.

Major uses of handouts:

▶ Provide the audience with a record of and the data from the presentation.

▶ Reinforce important information.

▶ Summarize action items for the audience to follow up on.

▶ Supply additional supporting data that you don't want cluttering up your spoken presentation or projected slides.

Once you have decided what handouts would be beneficial, you must then decide when you are going to hand them out. There are three choices: before, during, or at the conclusion of the presentation.

Before the Presentation

This is the preferred method in business presentations. Typically, copies of the slides are distributed. You can use the Speaker Notes function in Microsoft PowerPoint, or a similar function in other presentation software, so you can put a narrative explanation on the page with the slide copy.

Many speakers complain that audiences jump ahead and don't stay focused. This is not the fault of the handouts! It is the fault of the presenter, for not engaging the audience and managing their attention.

The main problem is that your audience might want to satisfy their curiosity about the contents of the handouts as you are speaking. When people are reading, they are not listening. One way to deal with this problem is to have the handouts in place when audience members enter the room. This will allow them to read the handouts before you begin speaking. In addition, you can explain the handouts before actually starting the presentation, thus satisfying people's curiosity about the contents.

Throughout this book you will find additional tips maintaining audience interest and focus.

During the Presentation

This must be done carefully. Handouts during a presentation must be distributed quickly and must be relevant to the point you are making. Otherwise, they will be a distraction, not an aid.

At the Conclusion of the Presentation

If the audience is accustomed to receiving handouts with presentations, or if it would be useful for them to follow the presentation with the data before them, you might not want to withhold the handouts. However, if handouts—such as glossy photos or marketing brochures—are going to distract from your oral presentation and not add substantially to the message, hold them until the end of the presentation.

Preparing For Your Next Presentation

Use this sheet to help prepare your next presentation.

For my presentation, I will:

- ❑ Clarify my presentation objectives.

- ❑ Analyze the audience.

- ❑ Develop my opening core message: Situation, Complication, Implication, Position, Action, and Benefit statements (SCIPAB).

- ❑ Brainstorm the main and supporting ideas.

- ❑ Add color spots, including slides.

- ❑ Develop my closing.

Using Slides and Other Visual Aids

"*If your words or images are not on point, making them dance in color won't make them relevant.*"

—Edward Tufte, Professor Emeritus, Yale University

In this part:

▶ Using Slides and Visual Aids Effectively

▶ Designing Your Slides

▶ Use Your Slides—Don't Let Them Use You

Using Slides and Visual Aids Effectively

If you want to be an increasingly successful presenter, the effective use of visuals can play an important part in achieving that goal. Slides, for example, if thoughtfully created and skillfully used, can greatly enhance a speaker's impact. Often, however, slides are included in ways that add little or actually detract from a presentation.

It is important to first have a well-thought-out strategy for your presentation and then to use slides as a tactical device to execute that strategy. Unfortunately, many presenters prepare their slides without creating a plan.

PowerPoint: *The features and steps listed in this part are specific to PowerPoint 2007. The discussion also applies to previous versions of PowerPoint, but the steps will be different.*

When Slides Help

Slides can significantly improve the persuasiveness of a presentation, as well as strengthen your ability to convey important information to the audience.[1] It is important, however, that you use slides for the purposes they serve best:

▶ Focusing your audience's attention

▶ Stimulating interest and attention

▶ Reinforcing key ideas or data

▶ Illustrating hard-to-understand information or data

▶ Increasing audience retention of your content

When They Don't

Many speakers use slides in ways that reduce, rather than enhance, a presentation's impact on the audience. You have probably witnessed presentations in which:

▶ Slides contained overwhelming amounts of detail

▶ Slide content and/or sequencing made too many points or no point at all

▶ Slides were used primarily to avoid audience interaction

Too commonly, the speaker reads the slides, making them the presentation, rather than using the slides as a visual aid that puts the speaker's relationship to the audience first.

---

[1] Management Information Systems Research Center, School of Management, University of Minnesota. *Persuasion and the Role of Visual Presentation Support: The UM/3M Study*. Minneapolis: University of Minnesota, 1986.

Let's Use Common Sense

PowerPoint and similar presentation software programs have become so flexible and easy to use that they are no longer just slide production tools but document production tools as well. "Missed the meeting? Let me send you my slides."

People find themselves creating business plans, strategic roadmaps, training materials, and product plans as PowerPoint presentations. Their slides become stuffed with supporting material that was never really intended to be displayed, but is displayed anyway. "I know you can't really read this slide but...."

Identify the Problem

When creating PowerPoint presentations, people run into two typical problems:

▶ **Putting all their notes on the slides**, instead of using separate speaker notes. Much of what ends up on the screen is really for the presenter, not for the audience.

▶ **Including supporting information or details** that probably belong in an appendix or a handout. This information might need to be in the slides (and hidden), but it does not belong on the screen.

Making these mistakes will greatly reduce your ability to connect with your audience and have a personal impact.

Choose a Solution

If you normally include extraneous information with your slides, consider the following solutions:

▶ Take those "notes" off the screen and put them in the Notes pane for each slide.

▶ Leave the detail on a slide, but "hide" that slide and show the audience a graphic or less detailed content to make your point.

▶ Keep slides that contain your notes hidden for future readers who may want the additional detail or who missed your presentation and received only the handouts. (In the Appendix, see "Some PowerPoint Tips and Tricks.")

The judicial use of slides will strengthen your message and the way your audience perceives you as a presenter. Plus, you'll be a step closer to achieving your ultimate goal of helping the audience understand and retain your key message.

As you've seen, slides can be either an asset or a liability to your presentation. The guidelines that follow will help you put your slides in the plus column.

Designing Your Slides

The problems created by crowded slides can be solved by applying some common sense to the slide design. You don't want your audience members so focused on trying to decipher the "eye charts" projected in front of them that they miss the key messages you are trying to get across. Yet this is a frequent occurrence. It is no wonder that the phrase "Death by PowerPoint" has come into our language.

A better alternative than the "eye chart" slide is to show only a clear summary, consisting of a line or two of content, a few bullet points, or some other visually appealing version of the handouts' essential points to support what is being said.

Here are a couple of tips for creating visually appealing slides:

▶ **Use the KISS rule.** As a guideline for producing visuals to support a presentation, remember the old KISS rule: **K**eep **I**t **S**hort and **S**imple. Ideally, the content of each slide should be understandable by persons who have only a basic knowledge of your topic.

▶ **Design all slides with common sense,** especially for slides with very technical content. Sometimes this simply means using a design that ensures that everyone in the room can easily read everything on the screen. This guideline alone can help you avoid the "Death by PowerPoint" syndrome.

The content of your slides also needs to be attractively and comprehensively arranged. This often requires common sense far more than artistic flair.

Estimating How Many Slides You Will Need

A big pitfall is trying to squeeze too many slides into a presentation. Don't automatically think that more is better. Often, the opposite is true.

You can calculate the approximate number of slides you should use for your presentation by allowing an average of two minutes of viewing time per slide, minimum. If your presentation includes complex diagrams or explanations, allow even more time per slide. This might mean using fewer slides than you first assumed was necessary.

Creating Your Titles

When creating your titles, keep the following in mind:

▶ **Each slide title should serve as a headline, not just a label.** The headline should be a short sentence with a verb. For example, "Our Computer Network Must Be Modernized" is a better title for communicating your message than just "Computer Network."

▶ **The headline should capture the slide's key "sound bite," or point.** Think of it this way: if someone were to walk into your presentation when you were halfway through discussing a particular slide, that person should be able to get the main point from reading the headline. Whenever possible, the title of a slide should state the conclusion you want the audience to reach or the action you want people to take.

▶ **Limit titles to two lines.** A subtitle might occasionally be appropriate as the second line to describe more precisely the content or central point of the slide. If you were to lay out your slides and read just the titles, the audience should understand what each slide is telling them.

▶ **Use a consistent capitalization style.** The most common practice is to use "title case," in which you capitalize only the first letter of each word, but don't capitalize articles, conjunctions, or prepositions. Another option is to use sentence case. Decide what capitalization style looks best for your content, and use that style consistently. Whatever you decide, don't use ALL CAPITALS because that may look like you're shouting!

Getting to the Point(s)

A sensible guideline for using bullet points on slides is the "five-by-five rule." Limit the content of each slide to a maximum of five bullet points (including any sub-points) and a maximum of five words per bullet. Or think of this rule as giving you around 25 words to play with, excluding the words in the title or graphics.

This rule enables your audience to glance at a slide's content and still pay attention to what you are saying. It also helps you avoid reading your slides to the audience (another pitfall that makes for dull presentations).

Exception: *Sometimes, to achieve clarity, you'll find that the temptation to break the five-by-five rule on a particular slide is too great to resist. In those cases, allow up to six words on some lines, and/or go to six lines on the slide if you must, but keep the total number of words on the slide to 25 or fewer.*

Here are a few other tips for making your slides look great:

► **Keep some white space between bullet points.** The easy way is to add a line break after each bullet point by placing the insertion point at the end of the line of text and pressing Shift+Enter. The better way is to learn how to change the default line spacing between bullet points by opening the Paragraph dialog box and changing the Spacing Before or Spacing After each bullet point.

► **Keep bullet points to a maximum of two lines**, never three if you can help it. You might need to reduce the font size a bit to do this, but never reduce font size to less than 24 points if possible.

► **Avoid sub-bullets whenever you can.** They can make you sound like you are reading the slide even if you're not. For clarity and appearance, don't put more than one level of sub-points under any bullet point, even though PowerPoint allows for up to four sub-point levels.

► **Hide your "note" slides.** You can retain those busy slides with way too many words on them, but don't show them in the presentation. Instead, hide them. They're there for you to use as notes or reference, for people who missed the presentation, or for anyone who will be presenting this content in the future.

► **Never read the slides to the audience.** Instead, discuss them, amplify on them, or comment on them. If you find yourself reading your slides to the audience, you undoubtedly have put too many words on the slides. Worse yet, whether your listeners say so or not, some (perhaps most) in your audience might be wishing that you had just sent them your slides, so they could read the slides for themselves without wasting their time.

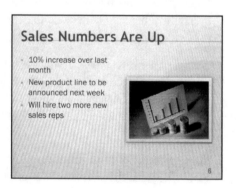

Sample presentation (first 6 slides of a 16-slide presentation)

Choosing the Right Words

> *The difference between the almost-right word and the right word is really a large matter—it's the difference between the lightning bug and the lightning."*

–Mark Twain

Spend the time required to carefully choose your words for each slide. If lengthy explanations, long sentences, or detailed descriptions are necessary, it's best to reserve those for your handouts.

For bullet points, avoid using full sentences. Use phrases and key words that quickly communicate the essence of each point without a lot of reading.

Keep the grammar and style of bullet points consistent, and use a parallel structure for each point on a slide. For example, this material:

▶ This PC is faster and cheaper than anything around

▶ Includes a color monitor

▶ Multimedia

…is better presented as:

▶ Fastest PC at this price

▶ Color monitor included

▶ Multimedia capability built in

Although some people like the look, capitalizing the first letter of every word in bullet points can cause some slides to look too busy and can make them more difficult to read. A common practice for bullet points is to capitalize only the first letter of the first word and the first letter of proper nouns. Decide what capitalization style works best for your purposes and use that style consistently throughout your slides.

At the Margin

The best practice is to use professionally designed templates that come with PowerPoint, are provided by your company, are downloaded from www.microsoft.com, or are purchased from third-party vendors.

If you change the template you are using, make sure you always leave at least a quarter-inch margin around all sides of every slide. The resolution of some LCD projectors and the size of the projection screen can cut off the image or make the edges of the display fuzzy.

Getting Fancy with Animations

Custom Animation, the feature that allows you to reveal a slide's bullet points and graphics one at a time, should be used only when absolutely needed—and this is not very often! The technique is greatly overused, and it can lead to the audience and the speaker spending too much time on the slide and not enough time interacting with each other. It forces the speaker to talk about every bullet point rather than give a summary statement.

Distractions

In addition, this technique is contrary to how adults like to process information and learn—they like to see or hear the big picture first, and then the detail. The slide that is shown all at once serves as a mini-agenda for that moment in time, making the audience more comfortable and less likely to interrupt with a question out of sequence. And to be blunt, many people find it boring or annoying to have each point revealed one after the other continuously throughout the presentation.

Rather than using animation on every bullet, reserve the use of the "build" slide to illustrate a process, a complex diagram, or a complicated chart. This will allow the audience members to follow your story as you divulge key aspects of the chart and pause to let them process the new information.

Getting Fancy with Transitions

Another trap to avoid is mixing different kinds of transition effects in the same presentation. Transition effects are the ways that your presentation moves from one slide to the next in Slide Show view. Using multiple slide transitions can be confusing and can draw attention away from your message.

Pick one transition effect or *No Transition* and use it throughout, unless you need a marked change to clearly define a shift between different sections of your presentation.

Numbering Slides

It's a good idea to number the slides for all presentations. Numbering enables audience members to refer to specific slides. It also enables the speaker to quickly move through the slides when it's desirable to go back to a previously covered slide to answer a question.

For virtual presentations, it's helpful to put a page number on every slide so you can refer your listeners to the slide you're discussing. On a teleconference call, listeners will sometimes be following along in "normal" mode and will welcome your reference to the slide number. The best way to add slide numbers to all the slides in your presentation is to use the Header and Footer dialog box.

Thumbnails

Never leave home without your thumbnails! In our research, we have found that many presenters see the advantage of being able to quickly find a particular slide by number or title. Print out a hard copy of your slides as thumbnails by performing these steps:

1. Open the Print dialog box.

2. Under Print what, select Handouts.

3. Under Handouts, in the Slides per page drop-down list, select 9 slides per page (or whatever number makes sense to you).

4. Click OK to print.

During your presentation, keep those printouts handy to use as a quick slide-number reference in case you choose to show a hidden slide or want to skip ahead or back to a specific slide during your presentation. (See the Appendix for additional PowerPoint tips and tricks.)

The Last Slide

It's not uncommon to accidentally hit the Down Arrow key (or whatever method you are using to move to the next slide) after the last content slide is shown in a presentation. When that happens, you will inadvertently end your presentation with an unintended result. To avoid this, add an "end" slide with a concluding phrase to use as the last slide in your presentation—just to be safe. Many presenters insert a blank slide or a logo slide, or they simply repeat their main title or introductory slide as their last presentation slide.

Using Colors

Your organization may have a preferred color scheme or template you'll be expected to use for your slides. If you need to change the background and text colors, use colors that have a high contrast. For example, white or yellow text on a dark blue background will be easier to read than the reverse.

It is usually best to limit the number of colors on a slide to between two and four to avoid a confusing rainbow effect. Decide what colors you'll use before you start creating your slides. This can save you considerable time in the long run.

Color Combinations for Images

▶ **Save yourself time and trouble:** When deciding on color combinations, use your software's color selection feature when you create several objects (such as boxes and circles) that require using more than two colors on a single slide. This feature is called *Theme Colors* in PowerPoint 2007 or *Color Scheme* in PowerPoint 2003.

▶ **Use colors for emphasis.** To highlight an object or text, make it a brighter color or simply add a shadow to it.

▶ **Apply colors to images consistently.** For example, if the same object is represented on several slides, use the same color for that object on all of your slides. This practice makes it easier for the audience to follow your ideas from slide to slide.

▶ **Consider people who are color blind.** Remember that a portion of the male population, and a smaller portion of women, has some degree of color blindness. Reds and greens will fade to grays for them. Use those colors only where gray would also be acceptable.

Color Placement

When deciding where to place various colors for objects on a slide, you can use the "earth-to-sky" theory,[1] remembering that the darker brown earth lies below the lighter blue sky. Following this visual principle—by having the colors of objects progress from darker at the bottom of the slide to lighter at the top (or from darker on the left to lighter on the right)—can make slides appear more balanced and pleasing to the eye. On the other hand, putting darker colors in the top tiers of a multi-tiered pyramid, for example, can make that graphic seem top-heavy and awkward.

Using and Choosing Fonts

A presentation generally reads better when only one or two fonts are used throughout. Calibri is the default font in PowerPoint 2007, and it conveys a somewhat conservative image. For a lighter but equally professional look, Arial is a popular font.

---

[1] Tom Mucciolo and Rich Mucciolo. *Purpose, Movement, Color: A Strategy for Effective Presentations.* New York: MediaNet, Inc., 2003.

```
This is Calibri
This is Arial
This is Verdana
```

Common Font Examples

Here are additional tips for using fonts in your slides:

► To highlight appropriate text, use **bold**, *italics*, or <u>underlining</u> rather than a different font.

► *Sans serif* fonts (fonts without strokes or "feet" at the ends of the letters) are easier and faster to read when projected on a slide. They are streamlined and uncluttered. Arial and Verdana are recommended sans serif fonts.

► The same font is commonly used for both a slide's heading and for its bullet points. You can use different fonts for each element if you prefer, but be sure the fonts are compatible in appearance.

► Use PowerPoint WordArt sparingly to highlight something or to make a point. Having too many such attention-getting items on a single slide is distracting.

Sizing Fonts

Whenever possible, use the default font size that is defined by the template. If you are going to reduce the font size, don't go below 20 points. If you must shrink the font size below 20 points to make all of your text fit, you probably have too much text on the slide, and there is a good chance that people will not be able to read it.

You might think that using a font size as big as 24 points looks huge on your computer screen:

This is 24-point Arial.

However, when this is projected as part of a slide on a screen, it will look much smaller, so don't be tricked by this optical illusion as you prepare your slides. This size will be fine when projected on the screen.

Remember: *The idea is to make sure that everyone in the room can read everything on the screen.*

Changing Colors and Fonts Globally

When you create slides in PowerPoint, it's best to select the appropriate *Slide Layout* for each slide and place your headings and bullets in the default title and text boxes that PowerPoint provides. Avoid any unnecessary use of the Text Box tool on the Drawing toolbar. This practice will make it easier for you to change all of the colors or fonts at one time, i.e., "globally," for the entire presentation.

To make global changes in your presentation, display the *Slide Master* view and make font and formatting changes on the Slide Master. For more information about the Slide Master and how to use it, use the PowerPoint Help system.

Moving Beyond Text

Drawings, animations, photos, embedded video clips, sound, and occasionally clip art can add life even to presentations on dry topics—but don't overdo it. Excessive use of any of these features can reverse the desired effect, distracting your audience and drawing listeners' attention away from what you are saying.

Caution: *Use any of the following devices only in ways that directly support your message. If they don't make your data, ideas, or conclusions easier to understand and believe, don't use them.*

Drawings and Animation

"A picture is worth a thousand words"… *sometimes!*

Pictures can break the monotony of showing slide after slide of bullet points. However, it is important to keep drawings and diagrams simple and to the point. Numerous boxes, lines, and arrows going every which way are bound to be confusing. Limit the use of boxes and circles, for example, to a maximum of eight on a slide.

A "drawn object" such as a box or a circle looks best in a single color. Such objects usually don't benefit from being outlined in a different border color.

Applying custom animation to drawings (displaying a slide in steps while in Slide Show view) is one of the simplest ways to keep an audience's attention. Once again, though, don't overdo it! While animation can help explain the flow of a complex process, too much animation keeps your audience waiting for the next visual trick instead of paying attention to what you are saying.

Always use animation that is appropriate to the object you are revealing. For example, use a left-to-right wipe for an arrow that is pointing in that direction; use a dissolve for a single object that you are revealing in successive stages. Limit animation sequences to two or three concurrent steps; otherwise, your audience is likely to get lost or confused.

Rather than describing the animation while it's playing, let the animation speak for itself; pause until it is complete before you start speaking again. Of course, if the animation is a lengthy one, speaking during its course will probably be necessary.

Clip Art

Use clip art very sparingly, if at all. Although clip art is an easy way to add pictures to boring text, its use (especially of cartoons that your audience may have seen many times before) can have a negative impact.

If you believe you must use clip art for some reason, avoid the standard clip art that comes with PowerPoint and other presentation software programs. You can access many Web sites offering less commonplace clip art, which can be purchased from the sites or even downloaded free for use in your presentation.

Make sure the clip art directly reinforces the content of your slide and is not just a picture for the sake of having a picture.

Photos

Compared to clip art, good photos can be enormously more appealing and more easily targeted to reinforce a specific point for the audience. You can supply the photos yourself from a digital camera or find them on the Internet.[1] If your existing photos are not already in a digital format, a scanner will allow you to easily incorporate those photos into slides.

Here are a few things to consider when using photos:

▶ **Trim the photo** to zero in on the part of the picture you want the audience to focus on. You do this by using the *Crop* tool in PowerPoint.

▶ **Make the picture fill two-thirds of the slide to add impact**, but only if it makes sense to do so and the resolution of the photo is high enough. You don't want to display an image that is grainy or pixelated.

▶ **Text on the picture must have a high contrast** with the background so that it can be easily seen and read by the audience.

---

[1] Cliff Atkinson. *Beyond Bullet Point: Using PowerPoint 2007 to Create Presentations that Inform, Motivate and Inspire*, Redmond, WA: Microsoft Press, 2007.

Video and Images

It is a good idea to edit your images, photos, or video clips to the size or resolution you want before you insert them into your presentation. Ideally, an image, photo, or video clip should take approximately one-half to two-thirds of the slide area, leaving adequate space for a title and description. Images, photos, or videos that are too small are often impossible to see clearly.

To insert a video clip in a PowerPoint 2007 presentation:

1. On the Insert tab, click the Movie button to open the Insert Movie dialog box.

2. Use the dialog box to navigate to the folder that contains the movie.

3. Double-click the movie file to place it on the slide.

4. A dialog box opens, asking you "How do you want the movie to start in the slide show," and there are two buttons to choose from:

   ▷ If you want the video to play when the slide is first displayed, click "Automatically."

   ▷ If you want the slide to be displayed first, and the video to play when you are ready, click "When Clicked."

To change how the video will play, activate the Animations tab and click the Custom Animation button to display the Custom Animation pane.

Sound

The appropriate use of sound can help make a point (for example, hearing the sounds of different engines in a presentation about the history of motorcars). Never use sound to be cute, clever, or funny. Incorporating a recorded testimonial, interview, or message from another person, however, can be an effective way to communicate a point.

If you plan to use sound, be sure the room is equipped for it. Speakers on a PC, for example, might be too small for the sound to be heard by the whole room. If the room has no sound system, and your PC speakers are inadequate, attach amplified speakers to the PC. In rooms with simple speaker facilities, you can usually put a regular microphone in front of the PC speakers to amplify the sound. In more sophisticated settings, a direct plug-in may be available to connect the computer to an amplified sound system wired in the room.

In all cases, when you're using sound, it is imperative to perform a sound check for the presentation—in the room you will be using—before the audience arrives. Experienced presenters also take the precaution of including text on the slide to communicate the point that they want the sound bite to make, just in case the sound system becomes inoperative for some reason.

Laser Pointers

You will want to stay out of the projector light when you are presenting. Resist the temptation to walk up to the screen and point at areas of the slide being displayed. Given that advice, you might be thinking it would be better to use a laser pointer. *However, laser pointers tend to be a major distraction and are simply not necessary in most business presentations.* Even though they are modern technology, the use of laser pointers is quickly becoming "old school."

The exception to this is an occasion when a laser pointer might be used to call attention to a very small detail in a chart or, more commonly, in a photograph. In general, always try to design the chart so that no laser pointer is needed. With photos, you don't have that option unless you can do a close-up, and if you can't, then the use of a laser pointer would be appropriate.

If you determine that you must use a laser pointer, first tell the audience what you are going to highlight. Then pause and point to it, using slow circles (which minimize the shaky hand syndrome). Begin speaking again only after you have made eye contact with the audience and lowered the laser pointer.

Using Material Created in Other Applications

Some of the content that you want to use in your presentation might exist in other formats, such as spreadsheets, text documents, Web pages, or charts. Embedding these files in your slides can save you the time and trouble of re-creating the material on a slide, but there are downsides.

Be aware. Unless you will open the file in full-screen mode in the application in which the file was created, be sure to keep in mind the following:

► The standard 10-point or 12-point font in a spreadsheet or document will not be readable on a slide.

► A chart with too many data points may be too small to see.

► The black text and white background typical of a spreadsheet or document may be hard to read in a large room.

For these reasons, it often makes sense to re-create the content you want to use in your slides, even when that content already exists in another application format. For example, you might need to display only the relevant portion of a table, not the whole spreadsheet. You can always include the full spreadsheet (or other detailed document) in your handouts, or link to it with an *Action* button or a *hyperlink*.

Use Your Slides—Don't Let Them Use You

There are some proven do's and don'ts that can make a big difference in the effectiveness of your entire presentation. Here are some of the most valuable:

▶ **Use the "B" key to black out the screen** (this works only in Slide Show view) during openings, closings, Q&A sessions, and extended discussions mid-presentation, as well as whenever you need to restore the speaker-audience connection.

▶ **Pause when looking at the screen.** Start talking only when eye contact is re-established. It is much better to look at the projected slide than at the laptop screen so you can stay in sync with the audience. The audience will be looking where you are looking. If you look at the laptop screen, they won't be able to see it.

▶ **Don't speak unless you are looking at your audience.** Look at your audience at least 95 percent of the time during your presentation, instead of looking at your slides or at your computer screen or keyboard. Simply pause for a moment when you look away.

▶ **Keep the room as fully lit as possible.** Keeping the lights on, as much as possible, is especially important in the afternoon when people are prone to snoozing.

▶ **If you have a portable screen, move it to the side and angle it 45 degrees to the audience.** That way, *you*—not the screen—will occupy center stage.

▶ **Talk about, discuss, and amplify the points on your slides.** Don't allow the slides to *become* your presentation simply because you are reading them to the audience. That is deadly dull. You want audience members to glance at a slide for just a second or two, "get it," and then put their full visual attention back on you.

▶ **Interact with your audience frequently and appropriately.**

Beware of Pop-Ups

Disable all instant messaging programs and e-mail preview pop-ups before you start a presentation. Messages and pop-ups can be distracting and sometimes embarrassing! Take your computer offline unless you need to access the network or the Internet for some reason.

Part Summary

Remember, the slides are not the messenger—you are. Your slides are just a communication aid, a tactical device to help you execute your overall presentation strategy.

Slides do not automatically have a positive impact. They can make a presentation clearer and more appealing, or they can muddy it up and distract your listeners.

The result you achieve depends on how effectively your slides are created and how well you use them.

Back Up Your Presentation: *It's always a good idea to back up your files. If you are traveling with a laptop, it's a good safety plan to carry your presentation on a separate drive, such as a USB flash drive (or "thumb drive"). If for any reason your laptop doesn't work or is lost, you can load your presentation onto another computer and be ready to go.*

Preparing for
Your Presentation

There are always three speeches, for every one you actually gave.
The one you practiced, the one you gave, and the one you wish you gave."

–Dale Carnegie

In this part:

▶ Personal Appearance

▶ Controlling the Presentation Environment

▶ When You Can't Practice—Successful Impromptu Speaking

Personal Appearance

This section is intended to provide not specific fashion guidelines but rather some general considerations on your dress and appearance. In general, avoid excess. Keep patterns, accessories, and colors simple. You should be the focus, not what you are wearing.

There is a growing trend toward casual dress in the workplace. "Business casual" has replaced suits for both men and women in many environments. For presentations, who is in the audience will always determine how you should dress. When in doubt, dress up a bit.

For Women

► **Clothes should fit well, but not too tightly.** If you're wearing a dress or skirt, choose the hem length based on what works for you and what you'll look like to those in the audience, especially if you are sitting up on a stage. Generally, longer sleeves are recommended to maintain a more business-like appearance.

► **Find two or three colors that work well with your complexion and hair color.** You might want to consult one of the many books on the subject or contact a "color consultant." You can then combine complementary accessories with your basic outfits to provide variety. Find good fabrics and make sure that they don't make noise when you move! Generally, avoid very bright reds and oranges, and avoid blacks and whites, because these colors are harsher and tend to draw attention away from the face.

► **Avoid jewelry that sparkles, dangles, or makes noise.** More subtle accessories are called for when you are the presenter. Large earrings, brooches, and bracelets that distract will annoy the audience and draw attention away from your presentation.

► **Makeup should be simple and flattering.** Overdone makeup can become the focus of negative, and unwanted, attention. Makeup that is well done can control oily areas of the face that might reflect light, enhance natural features, and help you look more relaxed in even the most difficult presentation situations.

► **Your hair style should be professional and controlled.** Longer hair worn loose can invite nervous gestures and be distracting to the audience. You want your audience to be watching your expressions, not your hair! In addition, keep hair off the face as much as possible. If a lock of hair tends to fall across your face, pin it back.

For Men

▶ **Casual wear and suits should be well tailored.** For presentations, clothes that are checkered or brightly colored, or that clash, will not reflect well on your image. Generally, dark blues, grays, and blacks in single- or double-breasted classic styles are the safest bet. Depending on the audience, a sport coat and well-matched trousers may do.

▶ **Men's suit coats are designed to be buttoned,** whereas many women's coats are not. In a presentation, depending on the level of formality, you may want to button the jacket, unbutton it, or take it off altogether.

▶ **Shirts should fit well, and the color should not be too bright.** If you are worried about perspiration showing, wear a cotton T-shirt and a white shirt. If you're appearing on TV, avoid white or patterned shirts, in favor of a solid light gray.

▶ **Ties can be used to complement the color of your eyes and face.** The traditional red "power tie" may not be the best color for you. Experiment a bit. The red tie causes the audience's eyes to focus first on the tie and not on you. Subtler colors may work better for you.

▶ **Shoes should be appropriate, comfortable, and well shined.** Make sure that your socks match and that they cover any bare leg when you sit down.

▶ **Hair frames the face.** It should be well groomed regardless of style. Beards should be well groomed also, and mustaches should be trimmed above the lip line.

▶ **If you're not sure how to dress for a particular meeting or presentation, ask someone who might know.** If you can't ask someone, make your best guess and then dress up one notch. You can always remove that tie, but if you don't have it and need it, you might be in trouble!

And a Word about Glasses for Both Sexes

The rule of thumb in presentations is to wear glasses if you need them to see your audience or read visuals. If you do need them, you might consider getting an anti-glare coating on the lenses. The coating eliminates possible glare and will allow others to clearly see your eyes. Also, avoid tinted lenses because they will increase the audiences' difficulty in seeing your eyes. Positive eye contact is always essential!

Controlling the Presentation Environment

A few minutes of planning, checking equipment, and arranging seating can prevent disasters. Presenters can usually exercise a degree of control over their speaking environments.

Kathleen

Kathleen worked all week preparing for her quarterly presentation. She has rehearsed (standing up and using her slides), and she feels prepared and confident. The morning of her presentation, she arrives early to go over her material one final time.

As she enters the meeting room for her presentation, Kathleen notices her manager and her department head in the audience. She is anxious but knows she is prepared. Kathleen took the time in advance of the presentation to make sure the LCD projector and her laptop worked well together and that the slides were displayed correctly.

She had too much riding on this presentation to do otherwise.

Items to think about before your presentation:

❑ **Computer hardware and software** — Always check hardware and software immediately before the presentation to make sure all systems are functioning. Have a backup plan in mind in case the equipment fails—remember Murphy's Law.

❑ **Flip chart** — Is there enough paper? Do you have a supply of marking pens? Have you checked to make sure the pens have not dried out?

❑ **Whiteboard** — Is the whiteboard clean and empty before you start the presentation? Also, do you have the proper markers and eraser for the whiteboard?

❑ **Handouts** — Are handouts easily accessible and in order, so they can be distributed with minimum disruption? Have you arranged for assistance in handing them out if needed?

❑ **Microphones** — If you're speaking to more than 50 people, you will probably need a microphone. Before your presentation, you may want to request a microphone that allows you to move around. Request a wireless lapel mic (or lavaliere microphone) that will hook on your jacket or tie and allow you to keep your hands free.

❑ **Lighting** — Try to leave on as much light as possible. Dimming the lights can contribute to people dozing off, especially after lunch.

❑ **Seating arrangement** — If you have control over seating in the room, use it. If possible, arrange the seating so that the exit and entrance to the room are in the rear. This way, if people come and go, it will cause the least amount of distraction.

If you know approximately how many people are going to be present, try to make sure that there are approximately as many seats as audience members. That way you won't have your audience sitting in the back of the room. Keeping your audience closer will focus their attention where you want it.

CHECKLIST FOR PRACTICING YOUR PRESENTATION

The following is a checklist for your practice sessions. Staying aware of these steps will help you give a more relaxed, confident, and enthusiastic presentation.

❑ **Don't read from your slides!** Remember, talk to the audience and explain, amplify, or discuss the slide content.

❑ **Mentally run through the presentation to review each idea in sequence** repeatedly until you become familiar with the flow of ideas and where you plan to use slides to support them.

❑ **Begin stand-up rehearsals of your presentation.** Try to arrange a practice room similar to the one in which you will actually give your presentation.

❑ **Give a simulated presentation**, idea-for-idea (not word-for-word), using all slides.

❑ **Strive for maximum focus on the audience**, minimum focus on the notes.

❑ **Practice answering the questions** you anticipate from the audience.

❑ **Give the full presentation again.** If possible, videotape yourself or have a friend give you some feedback.

❑ **Review the video and/or the friend's feedback** and incorporate any necessary changes.

❑ **Give one or two dress rehearsals of the presentation in its final form.**

When You Can't Practice— Successful Impromptu Speaking

Alex

Alex is invited, along with his manager, to attend a meeting of all department heads in the company. He is not expecting to say anything; he expects only to sit and listen. During his manager's presentation, he is asked a question about the department's plans for the coming year. His manager turns to Alex and says, "Alex, you've been working on our major project for the past year. Maybe you could say a few words about how this project got started, where it stands, and where it is going."

If something like this happens to you, do not panic! You already know the fundamentals of organizing your thoughts, and you know your job. With these two resources, you can effectively respond by taking the following steps:

Think

Quickly formulate a simple SCIPAB (Situation-Complication-Implication-Position-Action-Benefit) statement. Then, plug into a pattern of organization. Any topic can be split up into components. Before you speak, break your topic into a pattern such as:

▶ **Past, present, and future** or any time-oriented combination

▶ **Topics 1, 2, and 3** (e.g., production, advertising, and marketing)

▶ **Pros and cons** of an issue (useful in persuasive situations)

In Alex's case, the topic-ordered sequence is the best approach.

Then Speak

Start with your SCIPAB, and then state your key points. From the example above, Alex could simply state, "I would like to tell you about our production, advertising, and marketing departments."

Deliver the body of the presentation.

▶ **Talk through each point from your preview sentence.** Having an organizational pattern established and knowing where you are going will take some of the stress out of the situation.

▶ **Acknowledge the opposition.** If what you are speaking about is controversial, first acknowledge the opposition's case, but finish with your viewpoint so you end by summarizing your position.

▶ **Review the main points.**

▶ **Reinforce the main ideas you have touched upon** by briefly restating them. Say something like, "I've tried in these past few minutes to give you an overview of our key departments: production, advertising, and marketing."

▶ **Conclude the presentation.** Do not leave your audience high and dry. Conclude with a strong restatement of your position, action, and benefit.

Part Summary

As you prepare your presentation, remember to put into practice what you learned in this part:

1. Rehearse your presentation, standing up and using your slides.

2. Control the environment by checking:

   ❑ Computer hardware and software

   ❑ Seating arrangements

   ❑ Lighting

   ❑ Microphones

   ❑ Handouts

3. When asked to give an impromptu presentation:

   ❑ Develop a simple SCIPAB statement

   ❑ Plug into a pattern of organization

   ❑ Give a few introductory remarks

   ❑ Preview and review the main points for your audience

   ❑ Conclude with a strong restatement of position, action, and benefit

Delivering Your

Presentation

with Energy and

Composure

" *The human brain starts working the moment you are born and never stops until you stand up to speak in public.* "

–George Jessel

In this part:

- ▶ Engaging Your Audience
- ▶ Putting Energy to Work
- ▶ Maintaining Composure
- ▶ Question-and-Answer Techniques
- ▶ Dealing with Hostile Questions

Engaging Your Audience

You must communicate your enthusiasm to the audience if you want them to be enthusiastic about the ideas you present, and that takes energy. Simultaneously, you must appear composed and confident in your demeanor.

It's Not Just What You Say, But How You Say It

Standing stiffly, with little animation in your body, and speaking in a monotone voice without good eye contact is a sure way to deliver a speech that is a dud. We communicate with much more than words. Our nonverbal actions carry our feelings. If these channels get cut off because of anxiety, your interaction and rapport with the audience will suffer.

A great benefit of using a natural and animated presentation style is that your nervous energy will flow in a positive form and not stay in your body. Seek a natural, conversational style; relate to people in the audience in a direct and personable manner, as you would in a dialogue situation. Even in the most formal presentation situations, this is a necessity. You and the audience members are most familiar with dialogue behavior—not monologue behavior. So don't give the presentation in a stiff and unnatural manner.

You must learn to be aware of not only what you are saying but also how you are saying it. Learn to be your own coach while you are up in front of the audience, checking the items outlined in this section.

Putting Energy to Work

The following tips will help your presentation be animated, interesting, and engaging. If you can videotape a rehearsal, watch your delivery, looking for the following items.

Movement

Typically, speakers tend to stand in one spot, feet rooted like a tree to the ground. Taking an occasional step or two is highly recommended for a couple of reasons. First, it will help reduce anxiety by releasing tension. Second, some movement engages the audience's attention and helps them focus.

When you move, follow this principle: *Look, Move, Plant.*

▶ **Look** at the person whom you are going to move toward.

▶ Then **move**.

▶ Finally, **plant** your feet and stop moving.

If you keep moving, you will be pacing, and most people find that annoying.

If you are given a lectern to speak from, try to get away from it if possible. If appropriate, move to the side or front of the lectern to get nearer the audience. This position is more engaging, and audiences feel closer to the speaker without barriers in place. If you are using a microphone, you will need an extension cord or preferably a lapel mic. In a formal presentation, or if the lectern is at a head table, this technique might not be practical.

You should normally stay within four to six feet of the front row. Stay close, stay direct, and stay involved with your audience.

When delivering a presentation, keep your body facing the audience as much as possible. This will help you keep your eye contact with the audience, where it should be. Body orientation becomes critical when you're using slides. You will have to angle yourself away from the audience, but your body should not be angled more than 45 degrees. Don't speak to the slides. When you are not looking at the audience, simply pause. Speak only when you are looking at people.

Gestures

The importance of natural gestures, uninhibited by anxiety, cannot be overstated. Too often, anxiety holds back this important channel of communication. We use gestures for emphasis in normal conversation, without thinking about what we are doing with our hands.

Learn to gesture in front of an audience exactly as you would if you were having an animated conversation with a friend—nothing more, nothing less. Between gestures, simply relax your hands at your sides—do not hold them up in front of you with your arms bent at the elbow.

Using natural gestures will not distract from a presentation; however, doing one of the following certainly will.

What Not To Do

- ▶ Keep hands in your pockets.
- ▶ Keep hands "handcuffed" behind your back.
- ▶ Keep your arms crossed.
- ▶ Put hands in a "fig leaf" position (folding one hand over another, and letting the joined hands hang in front of the lower body).
- ▶ Wring your hands nervously.

Facial Expressions

Use the full range of appropriate facial expressions—and don't forget to smile!

Voice

You need to stay aware of your volume. A soft voice may be perceived as showing a lack of confidence and could hurt your credibility.

All vocal production starts with breathing. Breathe frequently and deeply to fuel your voice. When you speak, variety is the key. Vary your pitch, volume, and pacing, as you do in natural conversation or in storytelling. Your listeners will listen!

To find out if you have a volume problem before a presentation, ask someone who will give you a straight answer. Ask that person if you can be heard in the back of a room, if you trail off at the end of a sentence, or if you are speaking too loudly.

Too Soft?

If your problem is a soft voice, there is a simple exercise to learn how to increase your volume.

Recruit two friends to help you. Go into a room that is at least twice the size of the one where you normally give presentations. Have one person sit in the front row, and have the other stand against the back wall. Start speaking, and have the person in the back give you a signal when you can be heard clearly. Note your volume level. How does it feel? Check with the person in the front row to make sure you were not too loud.

Most monotone voices are caused by anxiety. As the speaker tightens up, the muscles in the chest and throat become less flexible, and air flow is restricted. When this happens, the voice loses its natural animation and a monotone results. To bring back the natural animation, you must relax and release tension. Upper- and lower-body movements are vital. The movement does not have to be dramatic—you need just enough to loosen the muscles and breathe normally.

Videotaping yourself, audio taping yourself, or getting feedback from a friend will let you know how you are doing.

Too Loud?

A voice that's consistently too loud sometimes indicates a slight hearing loss. If your voice is judged too loud, you might want to check with your doctor. If your hearing is okay, then do the above exercise again, but this time let the person in the front row give you a signal to soften your voice, and then check with the person in the back to make sure you can be heard.

When you have a large audience, it is appropriate to ask during a presentation, "Can you hear me in the back?" The audience will usually be honest because they want to hear what you are saying.

Maintaining Composure

Posture

Keep your posture erect, but relaxed. You want to stand up straight, without being stiff. Your weight should be evenly distributed. Don't place your weight on one hip, and then shift to the other and back again. This shifting can distract the audience.

Eye Contact

Speak to one person at a time when you present. Can you imagine interviewing a person who looked at the wall or floor when answering your questions? This would not inspire your confidence in that person.

In our culture, we expect good, direct eye contact. Yet in many presentations, a speaker will look at a spot on the back of the wall, or at a screen, or at notes—everywhere but into the eyes of the audience.

Note: *Eye contact is a big cultural variable, so always find out what the audience is comfortable with if you are presenting in a culture outside your own.*

Eye contact opens the channel of communication between people. It helps establish and build rapport. It involves the audience in the presentation and makes the presentation more personable. Good eye contact between the speaker and audience also helps relax the speaker by connecting the speaker to the audience and reducing the speaker's feeling of isolation.

Three to Five Seconds per Person

The rule of thumb for eye contact is three to five seconds per person. Try not to let your eyes dart around the room. Try to focus on one person, not long enough to make that individual feel uncomfortable, but long enough to pull him or her into your presentation.

Then move on to another person.

When you give a presentation, don't just look at your audience—see them. Seek out individuals, and be aware that you are looking at them.

If the group is large, make eye contact with individuals in different parts of the audience. People sitting near the individuals you select will feel as if you are actually looking at them. As the distance between a speaker and the audience increases, a larger and larger circle of people will feel your "eye contact."

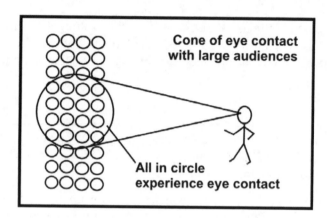

Pace

It's natural to speak more rapidly when we get nervous. The problem is that if you do so, you may look nervous, and like you are lacking confidence. In addition, if you are speaking too rapidly, audience members may miss an important point while their brains are processing the previous point.

An indication that you are talking too fast is tripping over words. When this happens, slow down. Listen for yourself to say the last word of a sentence, pause where the period would be, and then proceed to your next sentence. My advice is to slow down, listen to your own voice and make sure you are using a conversational pace, and pause as described next.

Pausing

Pausing during a presentation can be an effective device to allow your important points to sink in, and it can help you slow down if you are nervous. Don't be afraid to allow small periods of silence during your presentation. The audience needs time to digest what you are saying. The best places to pause are following any punctuation mark, such as a comma or period, just as you would leave a space there when writing. Use this time to take a breath and relax a moment.

Use a pause to fill those spaces that you might otherwise fill with sounds like "umm," "ahh," and "ah." A moment of silence will be a lot less distracting for your audience than those annoying verbal tics.

Learn to listen to yourself; stay aware not only of what you are saying but also of how you are saying it.

Question-and-Answer Techniques

Encouraging Your Audience to Ask Questions

Most presentations include time for audience questions during the session or at the end. In many cases, the speaker has the option of when to have questions asked. If this is the case, ask the audience to interrupt you whenever they have questions, or request that they save questions until you have finished the presentation. When you have delivered technical information or complicated ideas, or when you are leading a training session, it's a good idea to check audience comprehension by taking questions.

If you ask for questions passively, you will not encourage a response. This is often just a matter of body language. Standing away from the audience, hands stuffed in your pockets, and mumbling "Any questions?" does not encourage questions from an audience.

Speakers who actively seek questions will step toward the audience, raise a hand, and ask, "Does anyone have questions for me?" You might also ask, "What questions do you have?" You assume that the audience will ask questions, and they often do. Also, pause long enough after asking for questions so that the audience will have time to think of questions. (The silence should get to them before it gets to you!) Raising your hand will accomplish two things. One, it is the visual signal for questions and will encourage those who might be shy. Two, it helps keep order. Audience members will follow your lead and raise their hands, instead of yelling out their questions.

Listening Attentively to Questions

Perhaps you have seen a speaker listen to a question while pacing back and forth, not looking at the person who's asking the question. The speaker might not know what's being asked until the question is finished. It's important to wait until the questioner has finished.

While the question is being asked, you should watch the person who is asking it. Often it's possible to pick up clues about the intensity of the question, the feelings behind it, and any hidden agendas. Pay attention to the questioner's body language.

During questions, be careful what you do with your hands. Imagine giving a presentation enthusiastically and presenting your ideas confidently. Then imagine that when you receive a question, you stand looking at the floor, rubbing your hands together nervously. This behavior can negate the confident image you projected during the presentation. Your hands should stay in a neutral position, arms at your sides, fingers open. Focus on the question and listen carefully.

Answering Questions

Prepare for Questions

You should be able to anticipate most of the questions you receive. Practice answering them. Prepare for the worst, and everything else will seem easier. Some speakers prepare backup visual aids to be used specifically when answering anticipated questions.

Don't Preface Your Answer

When a speaker starts an answer with, "That's a very good question; I'm glad you asked it," it may be a sign that the speaker is unsure of the answer. At the end of your question-and-answer session, you can say something like, "Thank you for all your excellent questions."

Clarify

If the question you receive is lengthy or complex, restate it for clarification. This may not be necessary if the question is simple and straightforward. But sometimes, people are thinking aloud as they formulate their questions, and even the simplest inquiry may become confusing as it is buried in 17 paragraphs of commentary. Clarifying can also allow you to soften hostile language used in the question and give you more time to consider your answer.

Amplify

Have you ever been sitting in the back of an audience when someone in the front row asks a question and you can't hear it? If in doubt, you might want to repeat the question so that you are sure everyone heard it. This technique can also give you extra thinking time.

Maintain Your Style

When you're answering questions, it is important to maintain the same style and demeanor you used in the presentation. A change in demeanor can suggest that you are not confident about your position.

Be Honest

If you don't know the answer to a question, simply say, "I don't know the answer, but I will find out and get back to you." Or if co-workers might know the answer, you can ask them for help.

Involve the Whole Audience in Your Answer

Have you seen speakers who get involved with the person who has asked a question and ignore the rest of the audience? In some situations, the questioner might try to "hook" the speaker with a difficult question. You can always tell if a speaker is "hooked" because he or she focuses only on the person who asked the question.

Follow the 25%-75% Rule

Direct approximately 25% of your eye contact to the person who asked the question, and approximately 75% to the rest of the audience. (This guideline is especially important in a hostile question-and-answer situation.) Don't ignore the person who asked the question or the rest of the audience. Following this rule will help you stay in command of the situation and keep the audience involved in your presentation.

Keep Answers to the Point

Don't belabor an issue. Make your answer long enough to cover the subject, but short enough to be interesting.

Dealing with Hostile Questions

Let's face it, sometimes people in the audience are upset or angry, and they are going to take it out on you. It is probably one of the more difficult situations speakers face. Here is a proven three-step process for dealing with tough situations:

1. Align
2. Respond
3. Maintain

Align: Acknowledge Feelings and/or Facts

For example, someone might ask, "Why did you screw up and go 40 percent over budget?"

Using this technique, you would begin your answer by saying something like, "Mike, it's true; we did go over budget and I know you are upset about it." Notice that this reply is non-defensive, aligns with the questioner's beliefs or feelings, and avoids escalating hostility.

If you get defensive, you lose. Avoid saying something like, "I understand you're upset, but…." It is best to use some of the questioner's own language and to avoid saying the word "but." "But" tends to negate everything that came before it. Using some of the questioner's own language is the only proof the person has that you really heard him or her.

Respond: Respond with Information

At this point, explain what happened, with the facts of the situation. "As some of you may know, we had the opportunity to make a very large bid. In order to prepare the bid, we had to purchase five new computer systems. I am happy to report that it was an excellent investment, albeit over budget, because we won the bid."

Maintain: Maintain Your Position

For the final piece, it is imperative that you restate your original position, action, or benefit sentence so you finish with a strong statement of your stance on the issue. You can say something like, "That is why it is so important for us to increase the budget on this project."

Part Summary

As you prepare to deliver your next presentation with energy and composure, plan to:

- ❑ Stay aware of not only what you say, but also how you say it.
- ❑ Be animated, enthusiastic, and direct in your delivery.
- ❑ Use eye contact to make your presentation personable and conversational, if that will work in your culture.
- ❑ Keep a clear, strong voice; do not speak too fast; and pause frequently.

Question-and-Answer Techniques

Also, plan ahead for questions by using these techniques:

- ❑ Ask for questions by stepping forward with a hand raised when you need to encourage questions.
- ❑ Anticipate questions and practice the answers.
- ❑ Watch the questioner and listen carefully to the question.
- ❑ Keep your hands in a neutral position, and don't back up when listening to questions.
- ❑ Repeat the question to make sure everyone heard it or to clarify it if necessary.
- ❑ Keep the same style and demeanor that you had during the presentation.
- ❑ Use eye contact and involve the whole audience in your answer.
- ❑ Use the Align-Respond-Maintain model for difficult questions.

A P P E N D I X

Appendix to Part 3

Some PowerPoint Tips and Tricks

In addition to the many PowerPoint suggestions mentioned in this section, try these presenter-proven tips:

1. When giving a presentation:

   ▷ If you want to **skip ahead or go back to a slide**, you can key in the slide's number and press *Enter* to navigate directly to that slide.

   ▷ **Hidden slides** are useful for storing content that you don't plan to use in the main body of the presentation but might need in certain circumstances. Depending on time constraints, the nature of the audience, and/or the direction of the discussion or questions, you might choose to show a hidden slide.

   One way to hide a slide is to view the presentation in either *Normal* or *Slide Sorter* view, right-click the slide you want to hide, and choose *Hide Slide* from the shortcut menu.

   A hidden slide is not shown in *Slide Show* view unless you choose to reveal it. To show a hidden slide in Slide Show view, key in the number of the slide and press *Enter*.

2. When creating a presentation:

   ▷ Decide on the **slide template** you will use *before* doing any custom formatting or adding multimedia. The *Presentation Designs* and sample templates provided in PowerPoint may help you formulate your ideas. (To see the templates, click the Office button and choose New. The New Presentation dialog box will open, and the template categories will be listed in the left pane.)

   ▷ To save time, learn the **keyboard shortcuts** for the most commonly used PowerPoint commands. These are usually highlighted in reference books. You will find that many of these keyboard shortcuts are universal to various Microsoft (or Windows-based) applications (e.g., Copy = Ctrl+C).

   ▷ If you will be **creating a number of drawn objects**, copy and paste from those that already exist on other slides whenever possible, instead of re-creating the objects each time. In addition to saving you time, this process will help ensure consistency throughout your presentation. Remember, however, that when you copy an object in PowerPoint and paste it onto another slide, the object will be placed in exactly the same position it was in on the original slide.

▷ To make sure your **drawn objects line up**, activate the View tab. In the Show/Hide group, check Gridlines and then draw the object. By default, the *Snap to Grid* feature is active and ready for you to use. Here are some ways to do that:

— As you move a drawn object near a grid line, the object will snap into place.

— Press and hold Shift and then drag to *move* objects in a straight line.

— Press and hold Shift+Ctrl and then drag to *copy* objects in a straight line.

To customize the Snap to Grid options, select the drawn object and activate the Drawing Tools | Format tab. Then click the Align button to display the drop-down menu, and choose Grid Settings to open the Grid and Guides dialog box. Make the necessary changes and click OK.

▷ When **inserting graphics** from other applications, be sure you choose the correct file format so the graphic will be displayed and printed correctly. Also, keep the following tips in mind:

— For bitmap images such as photos, save your graphics as Tagged Image Format (.tif) with LZW compression; JPEG (.jpg) with medium to high-quality resolution; or bitmap images (.bmp), although bitmaps can tend to produce larger file sizes.

— To decrease the size of your photo file, set the resolution to 100 to 150 dots per inch (dpi). Any lower resolution will make the graphic look blurry.

— Avoid inserting Encapsulated PostScript (.eps) graphics. They print well, but they often are not displayed well on screen.

— Before sending your graphics to a service bureau, be sure to set your graphics to RGB color if you want transparencies, or to CMYK color if you want printed paper copies.

▷ When **resizing an image or bitmap,** press and hold Shift, and drag a corner resize handle to reduce or enlarge the image. When you do, the image will resize proportionately. If an image is too small and is blurry when enlarged, try cropping the image before enlarging it.

Additional Reading

Alley, Michael. *The Craft of Scientific Presentations: Critical Steps to Succeed and Critical Errors to Avoid.* Springer-Verlag, 2007.

Altman, Rick. *Why Most PowerPoint Presentations Suck.* Harvest Books, 2007.

Bunzel, Tom. *Solving the PowerPoint Predicament: Using Digital Media for Effective Communication.* Addison-Wesley, 2006.

Davis, Martha. *Scientific Papers and Presentations, 2nd Edition.* Academic Press, 2005.

Duarte, Nancy. *slide:ology: The Art and Science of Creating Great Presentations.* O'Reilly Media, 2008.

Tufte, Edward R. *Envisioning Information.* Graphics Press, 1994.

Tufte, Edward R. *The Cognitive Style of PowerPoint: Pitching Out Corrupts Within, 2nd Edition.* Graphics Press, 2006.

Tufte, Edward R. *The Visual Display of Quantitative Information.* Graphics Press, 2001.

Wempen, Faithe. *PowerPoint 2007 Bible.* Wiley Publishing, 2007.

Wilder, Claudyne and Jennifer Rotondo. *Point, Click, and Wow!* Jossey-Bass/Pfeiffer, 2007.

Zelazny, Gene. *Say It with Charts: The Executive's Guide to Visual Communication.* McGraw-Hill, 2001.

50-Minute™ Series

If you enjoyed this book, we have great news for you.
There are more than 200 books available in the
Crisp Fifty-Minute™ Series.

Subject Areas Include:

Management and Leadership
Human Resources
Communication Skills
Personal Development
Sales and Marketing
Accounting and Finance
Coaching and Mentoring
Customer Service/Quality
Small Business and Entrepreneurship
Writing and Editing

For more information visit us online at

www.CrispSeries.com